BREAKING THE ICE

The Ultimate Guide to Starting Conversations with Strangers

ELIZABETH ANDERSON

TABLE OF CONTENTS

INTRODUCTION

A helpful manual called "BRERAKING THE ICE" was produced to assist readers in overcoming their shyness and nervousness when it comes to speaking with strangers. The book, written by a seasoned communication specialist, offers advice on how to strike up conversations with strangers in a range of situations, including networking meetings and social gatherings.

The book begins with an explanation of why it can be difficult to strike up a conversation with a stranger and why it's vital to get past this anxiety. The discussion then moves on to specific methods for making a good impression, such as icebreakers, open-ended questions, and nonverbal cues.

The book also explains how to maintain a discussion by listening intently, replying wisely, and discovering points of agreement with the other party. It also offers suggestions on how to leave a conversation politely when it's time to move on.

All things considered, "BREAKING THE ICE" is a valuable tool for anyone wishing to develop their communication abilities and widen their social circle.

CHAPTERS

The Importance of Small Talk

Overcoming Fear and Anxiety

Finding Common Ground

The Art of Listening

Using Body Language

Managing Awkward Moments

Keeping the Conversation Going

Navigating Cultural Differences

CHAPTER 1

THE IMPORTANCE OF SMALL TALK

Small talk, which is frequently thought of as light, casual conversation between individuals, is actually a crucial component of social interaction. Although if it might not always result in lengthy or meaningful conversations, it still performs a number of crucial tasks for us every day. The following justifies the significance of small talk:

Relationships are formed and maintained through small chat, which is a powerful tool. It enables intimate connections between people and contributes to the development of trust and familiarity. People can get to know one another better, find things in common, and lay the groundwork for future talks through small chat.

Relationships are built through small chat, especially between persons who may not be very familiar with one another. People may feel more at ease and open to discussing their thoughts and feelings if boundaries are broken down and a pleasant environment is created.

INTEREST-REVEALING: Making small talk with someone demonstrates your interest in them personally. It shows that you are willing to put forth the effort to get to know them, which may pave the way for later, more in-depth, meaningful conversations.

ENHANCES CONVERSATIONAL ABILITIES: Engaging in small chat is an excellent method to practice communication skills including asking and answering questions, listening, and speaking clearly. These abilities can be helpful in both personal and professional contexts, spanning all facets of life.

REDUCES STRESS: In settings when people might feel embarrassed or uncomfortable, small chat can help to lessen stress and anxiety. People may feel more at ease as a result of it as it can assist to break the ice and foster a more laid-back environment.

Small chat can serve to foster a sense of community, especially in workplaces or other group settings. People may feel closer to one another and to the greater group or community as a result.

In conclusion, while small talk may seem like a trivial aspect of our everyday lives, it actually plays a crucial function in creating rapport, fostering connections, demonstrating interest, enhancing communication skills, lowering stress levels, and fostering a feeling of community. Hence, keep in mind that small talk is a crucial tool for social connection the next time you find yourself engaging in idle conversation with someone.

CHAPTER 2

OVERCOMING FEAR AND ANXIETY

An individual's health and ability to function on a daily basis can both be greatly impacted by the emotions of fear and anxiety. Even while it's normal to occasionally feel these emotions, continuous fear and worry can become crippling and interfere with day-to-day activities. People can, however, employ a variety of techniques to get over their fears and anxieties.

DETERMINE THE CAUSE OF YOUR FEAR AND ANXIETY

Finding the source of your fear and anxiety is one of the first stages to overcoming them. In order to properly regulate these emotions, people might create coping mechanisms by becoming aware of what causes them.

CONFRONT YOUR NEGATIVE IDEAS

Negative thoughts that engender a sense of dread and gloom frequently fuel feelings of fear and anxiety. It's crucial to confront these thoughts and swap them out with more constructive ones if you want to get over these emotions.

PRACTICE BREATHING EXERCISES

People can lower their levels of anxiety and terror by using relaxation techniques such progressive muscle relaxation, deep breathing, and meditation. These methods can aid in calming racing thoughts and encouraging a state of peace and relaxation.

REGULAR EXERCISE

Frequent exercise has been demonstrated to lower stress and anxiety levels by causing the body's natural feel-good hormones, endorphins, to be released. Moreover, exercise can help with sleep, which is crucial for lowering anxiety and enhancing general wellbeing.

ASK YOUR RELATIVES AND FRIENDS FOR HELP

Speaking with friends and family members about worries and fears might give people a fresh outlook on their circumstances. Those who feel alone or isolated in their struggles may find this to be of particular benefit.

EXAMINE GETTING THERAPY OR COUNSELING

The use of therapy or counseling can help people overcome their fear and anxiety. A qualified therapist can assist people in locating the source of their worries and anxieties and creating unique coping mechanisms.

EXERCISE SELF-CARE

Self-care entails looking after one's physical, psychological, and emotional needs. This can involve doing things like maintaining a healthy diet, getting adequate sleep, maintaining decent cleanliness, and taking part in enjoyable and fulfilling activities.

Finally, overcoming fear and anxiety necessitates tolerance, perseverance, and a willingness to explore novel approaches. People can successfully control these emotions by recognizing their sources, confronting unfavorable ideas, using relaxation techniques, exercising frequently, asking for help from friends and family, thinking about therapy or counseling, and engaging in self-care.

CHAPTER 3

FINDING COMMON GROUND

Finding common ground with strangers is a crucial ability that can aid in connecting with them and developing a good rapport. Here are some pointers to help you strike up a conversation with a stranger:

ASK OPEN-ENDED QUESTIONS:
Open-ended questions are a great way to start a conversation and get to know the other person better. Open-ended inquiries nudge the respondent to divulge more about themselves, and their responses can reveal shared passions.

When the speaker starts, pay close attention to what they are saying. By nodding, making eye contact, and asking follow-up questions, you can demonstrate that you are interested. Active listening can help you find common ground by allowing you to pick up on cues that reveal shared interests.

FIND COMMONALITIES:

As the conversation develops, seek for ways in which your interests and experiences and those of the other person are comparable. If both of you enjoy hiking, for instance, you may discuss your preferred hikes, camping trips, or equipment.

DISCOVER SIMILAR EXPERIENCES:

Finding common ground can be facilitated by sharing experiences. You can discuss your common experiences, viewpoints, and observations if you both happen to be at the same event, for instance.

BE CURIOUS AND OPEN-MINDED:

You need to be curious and open-minded about the other person's experiences, opinions, and viewpoints in order to establish points of commonality. Approach the conversation with a genuine curiosity in learning more about the person and avoid making any assumptions or snap judgments.

Establishing a connection and finding common ground can be facilitated by sharing personal experiences. If the other person states that they like to travel, you could want to share your own trip tales, preferred locations, or travel advice.

Finally, maintain your optimistic outlook and concentrate on bridging any disagreements. Avoid divisive or difficult themes that can cause the conversation to veer off course and look for chances to connect with others.

In conclusion, finding common ground while conversing with strangers entails being curious and open-minded, actively listening, asking open-ended questions, seeking out commonalities, discovering shared experiences, sharing your own experiences, and remaining positive. You may connect with the person you are conversing with and develop a good relationship by following these strategies.

CHAPTER 4

THE ART OF LISTENING

The ability to fully concentrate on and understand what someone else is saying is the art of listening. It is an essential talent for good relationship-building and communication. Some essential components of the skill of listening include the following:

PAY ATTENTION:
To listen well, you must put your attention on the speaker and tune out outside noise. Maintain eye contact, pay the speaker your entire attention, and refrain from multitasking.

BE PATIENT:
Paying attention calls for tolerance and a willingness to hear the other person out. Provide them uninterrupted time to fully share their views and opinions.

Ask clarifying questions to make sure you comprehend what the speaker is saying. This demonstrates your interest in what they have to say and your active listening skills.

AVOID FORMING ASSUMPTIONS:

Refrain from drawing hasty judgments or presuming to know what the speaker is trying to say. Instead, give them a sympathetic ear while attempting to comprehend their viewpoint.

Put yourself in the speaker's position and try to comprehend their thoughts, feelings, and emotions. Your relationship with them will deepen and your trust will grow as a result.

Immediately following the speaker's completed speaking, correctly react. In order to do this, you may offer suggestions, talk about your own ideas or experiences, or just acknowledge what they're saying.

This involves paying close attention to the speaker and paraphrasing what they say. This demonstrates that you are paying attention and comprehending what they are saying.

In conclusion, listening effectively is an essential ability for effective communication and developing enduring connections. You can improve your listening and communication skills by paying attention, being patient, clarifying, avoiding assumptions, empathizing, reacting correctly, and engaging in active listening.

CHAPTER 5

USING BODY LANGUAGE

When conversing with strangers, using body language effectively can be a powerful tool. Here are some pointers on using body language to make a good first impression and build rapport with a new acquaintance:

The universal symbol of friendliness and approachability is a grin. When you first meet someone, look them in the eye and grin sincere. This will put them at ease and aid in breaking the ice.

Eye contact is crucial for effective communication because it conveys your interest in what the other person is saying. Maintain eye contact while talking to a stranger, but avoid staring or making them feel uncomfortable.

Keep your arms uncrossed and your body facing the person you are speaking to when using open body language. This demonstrates that you are receptive to the discussion and ready to pay attention.

Mirroring the body language of the other person can help to build rapport and foster a sense of connection. They can lean forward, and you can follow suit. You can mimic their hand gestures if they do so while speaking.

Pay attention to your posture because it might give you a more assured and self-assured appearance. Put your chin up, shoulders back, and your body straight.

EMPLOY THE RIGHT GESTURES:
Gestures can be an effective approach to highlight what you're saying and increase the recall of your message. But make sure your motions are suitable,

consistent with your message, and don't take attention away from what you're saying.

Avoid fidgeting because it can indicate anxiety or discomfort, which can make the other person uncomfortable. Try to remain still and pay attention to what is being said.

Ultimately, being able to read someone's body language well can help you build a strong rapport with them. You may establish rapport and improve the conversation for both of you by being conscious of your own body language and mirroring that of the other person.

CHAPTER 6

MANAGING AWKWARD MOMENTS

It can be intimidating to interact with strangers, especially when unexpected or embarrassing situations occur. You can learn to handle these circumstances with confidence and elegance, though, with a few straightforward tactics and some practice.

KEEP YOUR COOL:

When confronted with an embarrassing situation, it's critical to maintain your composure. Remind yourself that it's simply a temporary ache by taking a deep breath. Avoid letting your anxiety overpower you.

EMPLOY HUMOR:

Laughter is a great way to release tension and brighten the atmosphere. Try to find a method to make light of the situation if you ever find yourself in an uncomfortable one. A clever remark or joke delivered just so can help to ease tension.

Engage in active listening when conversing with strangers in order to fully understand what they are saying. This will make it easier for you to recognize clues and modify your answers accordingly. Also, active listening will enable you to communicate to the other person that you are interested in what they are saying.

BE TRUTHFUL:

It's acceptable to admit when you don't understand something or are in a scenario where you aren't sure how to react. You might say, "I'm sorry, but I'm not sure how to respond to that," or "Could you kindly explain that to me?"

If you're having trouble coming up with a topic to discuss, attempt to discover some common ground. Search for shared experiences or interests that both of you can relate to. This may enable you to establish a rapport with your listener.

Like anything else, navigating uncomfortable situations while conversing with strangers requires practice. Strive to place yourself in circumstances where you must frequently engage with strangers. Your comfort and confidence in your capacity to manage these situations will grow with time and experience.

The key to handling uncomfortable situations while chatting to strangers is to maintain your composure, use humor, listen intently, be honest, seek out common ground, and practice. You can manage difficult situations with confidence and ease if you keep these tactics in mind.

CHAPTER 7

KEEPING THE CONVERSATION GOING

It might be difficult to maintain a conversation with new people, especially if you're shy or introverted. Yet, you can master the art of small talk and maintain a seamless conversation with a little practice and a few useful hints. Here are some suggestions to help you continue a conversation with a stranger:

Begin by introducing yourself and extending a greeting: Introduce yourself and ask for their name to start. It's simple to start a conversation with the words "Hello, my name is [name], what's yours?"

POSE OPEN-ENDED INQUIRIES:
Pose questions that call for more information than a simple yes or no. Try asking "What do you think of this place?" as an alternative to "Do you enjoy this place?" This can make the conversation more

fascinating and offer the other person a chance to express their feelings.

Active listening after paying close attention to what the other person is saying, make any necessary follow-up remarks or inquiries. This will encourage them to continue talking by demonstrating your interest in what they have to say.

Seek out similar ground Search for shared experiences or interests between the two of you. This may be a wonderful method to connect with someone and maintain the conversation. If both of you enjoy hiking, for instance, you might inquire as to their favorite paths or discuss your personal hiking adventures.

BE UPBEAT AND ENTHUSIASTIC:

Having a positive outlook can help to keep the conversation moving. Try to have a cheerful and cheery tone while expressing passion and interest in what the other person is saying.

Don't be hesitant to express your own ideas and experiences. This can keep the conversation in check and demonstrate your willingness to engage with them and communicate.

Body language is important, so be aware of both your own and the other person's. To demonstrate that you are interested in the conversation, make eye contact, smile, and utilize the right body language.

Remember that being sincere, cordial, and curious are the keys to maintaining a conversation with strangers. You may develop deep relationships with individuals and reap the benefits of engaging in fruitful discussion with a little effort and practice.

CHAPTER 8

NAVIGATING CULTURAL DIFFERENCES

While conversing with strangers, navigating cultural differences can be difficult but rewarding. It calls for knowledge of cultural norms and the capacity to adjust to novel and unfamiliar circumstances. Here are some pointers for overcoming cultural barriers when conversing with strangers:

DO YOUR HOMEWORK:

It's crucial to learn about other cultures before interacting with strangers from them. This can aid in your understanding of their traditions, principles, and modes of communication. Seek up details online, speak with others who are familiar with the culture, or read books and articles on it.

BE RESPECTFUL:

Respect the culture and beliefs of the other person. Be aware of your facial expressions, tone of voice, and body language. Keep your assumptions and generalizations free of biases and preconceptions.

BE PATIENT:

Due to language difficulties, varying communication styles, and cultural variations, communicating across cultures can occasionally be difficult. Be patient and give the other person your complete attention as they speak. Don't start their sentences for them or finish them for them.

EMPLOY PLAIN LANGUAGE:

To prevent misunderstandings or confusion, use language that is straightforward and simple. Avoid using slang or idioms that could be foreign to the other person and speak slowly and clearly.

POSE INQUIRIES:

As a sign of interest and to better grasp the viewpoint of the other person, ask questions. Asking questions that can be regarded as intrusive or disrespectful in their culture is best avoided.

BE ADAPTABLE:

Be prepared to follow the other person's communication preferences and cultural customs. Be willing to take what you can from them and modify your own actions as necessary.

Be mindful of non-verbal cues because they can differ greatly between cultures. Examples include gestures and facial expressions. Be conscious of these variations and make an effort to modify your own nonverbal communication to more closely resemble the other person's.

Be considerate of others' personal space. Personal space differs between cultures. Be mindful of the privacy of others and make an effort not to encroach.

AVOID FORMING ASSUMPTIONS:
Steer clear of making assumptions about other people's cultures that are based on stereotypes or generalizations. Instead, concentrate on getting to know them personally.

Last but not least, be considerate of cultural differences and refrain from forcing your own cultural standards or ideas on others. The diversity that cultural variations provide to our world should be embraced and celebrated.

CONCLUSION

The book "BREAKING THE ICE" provides helpful pointers and guidance on how to approach and communicate with individuals you don't know. The necessity of establishing a good first impression, demonstrating sincere interest in other people, and identifying points of connection are all emphasized in the book.

It addresses issues including body language, conversation starters, and getting over social anxiety and shyness. Overall, the book offers helpful tips for establishing rapport and forging deep connections with strangers.